THE STRANGE HOUSE TESTIFIES

Bilingual Press/Editorial Bilingüe

Publisher
Gary D. Keller

Executive Editor
Karen S. Van Hooft

Associate Editors
Adriana M. Brady
Brian Ellis Cassity
Amy K. Phillips
Linda K. St. George

Address
Bilingual Press
Hispanic Research Center
Arizona State University
PO Box 875303
Tempe, Arizona 85287-5303
(480) 965-3867

THE STRANGE
HOUSE TESTIFIES

poems by

Ruth Irupé Sanabria

Bilingual Press/Editorial Bilingüe
Tempe, Arizona

Library of Congress Cataloging-in-Publication Data

    Sanabria, Ruth Irupé, 1975–
      The strange house testifies / Ruth Irupé Sanabria.
      p. cm.
    ISBN-13: 978-1-931010-50-4 (pbk. : alk. paper)
    ISBN-10: 1-931010-50-1 (pbk. : alk. paper)
    I. Title.

    PS3619.A487S77 2007
    811'.6—dc22

                          2007036795

PRINTED IN THE UNITED STATES OF AMERICA

Front cover art: Only One of You Shall Not Betray Me (1999) by Sonya Fe

Cover and interior design by Bill Greaves, Concept West

Acknowledgments appear on p. ix.

A Isai y a Raquel

CONTENTS

I. THE STRANGE HOUSE TESTIFIES

II. THE ADVENTURES OF GHETTO GIRL

III. CAN WE RECONCILE?

PERMISSIONS AND SOURCE ACKNOWLEDGMENTS

Excerpts from *Nunca Más: The Report of the Argentine National Commission on the Disappeared.* Copyright © 1986 by Writers and Scholars International Ltd. Reprinted by permission of Farrar, Straus and Giroux, LLC.

Grateful acknowledgment is made to the following journals and anthologies in which some of these poems first appeared:

Are All the Women Still White? Globalizing Women's Studies: "Hija."

CALYX, a Journal: "Papi's Afro Pick."

Coloring Book: An Eclectic Anthology by Multicultural Writers: "The Adventures of Ghetto Girl: At the D.C. Multiplex."

Long Shot: "The Strange House Testifies."

Poesía y derechos humanos: "Retrato de un padre—bahía blanca, 1977." Translation of "Portrait of a Father—Bahía Blanca, 1977" by Alicia Partnoy.

Poets Against the War: "Ten."

Signs: "Now for the Evening News."

U.S. Latino Literature Today: "Las a-e-i-o-u's de los ums seeking tongues of migratin' letras que ain't no way hiding."

Women Writing Resistance: "Las a-e-i-o-u's de los ums seeking tongues of migratin' letras que ain't no way hiding."

I

THE STRANGE
HOUSE TESTIFIES

THE STRANGE HOUSE TESTIFIES

No, Your Honor,
they did not pray the rosary,
they did not eat rice and beans.

Oh, they *ate* rice. But with butter.
And parmesan. A lot of parmesan.
And a lot of red meat.

I'm sorry, Your Honor,
could you please repeat the question?

Yes, they danced salsa.

With all due respect, Your Honor,
this *is* Washington DC . . .

I'm sorry. Yes.
They ate with
men loving men.

No, they did not cover their furniture in plastic.

No, never hung portraits of family
or images of Jesus on the wall.

They hung paintings and political poster art.

Of Eva Perón, The Head of Boaz
at Ruth's Feet, ni olvido ni perdón.*
Those sorts of things.

I'm sorry, I don't understand the question.

I'm sorry, I still don't understand the question.

Oh. A lot of Rubén Blades,
and songs like "¿Qué hicistes abusadora?"
and "Feeling Hot Hot Hot!"

They did, Your Honor. Mostly Heinekens
and red wines. Once in a blue moon, a white.

Certainly. I'll explain.
For the record:
across the entire length of my downstairs
first floor right wall
they painted in bold white letters
"FMLN VENCERÁ" "U.S. OUT OF PANAMA."

No, they were not drunk when they did that.

No, Your Honor, I do not believe they are alone.

It was the eldest girl, Your Honor.

She painted my 2nd bedroom door,
located on the 2nd floor facing east,
black.

Yes, she is also responsible for the
spray-painted anarchy sign on the ceiling.

Yes, that is true.
Her parents did not permit her to speak English in the house.

No, Your Honor, my relationship to this family was strictly a housing
deal.

---

* An Argentinean slogan, often associated with the Montoneros (an Argentinean political
organization), that refers to never forgetting nor forgiving the military and other respon-
sible parties for the deaths and disappearances of thousands of Argentineans prior to
and during the genocidal military dictatorship that began in 1976.

4

who's talking
who's being talked to
what questions do you imagine the judge asking.
what's about?

ARGENTINE FAMILY REJOICES

Title and nonitalicized excerpts from the Seattle
Post-Intelligencer, *Sunday, December 23, 1979.*

The three met again
in a leaping embrace
shortly before 9 PM
at a crowded National Airlines concourse.
The solemn-faced,
curly-headed little girl
reached out small hands
to clutch at her father
as they swirled around together.

> *we ran off that plane, fire chasing our bones.*

His wife was white of face
after 26 hours in flight.

> *plinkplunk plinkplunk!*
> *ribs and cheekbones*
> *nose and elbows*
> *plinkplunk plinkplunk!*
> *here she comes,*
> *a skeleton*
> *plinkplunk plinkplunk!*
> *carrying her fat, her fat*
> *and rosy daughter.*
> *plink pluck plink!*

Earlier, Mr. S—— carrying a bouquet
of red and white carnations—
had paced the concourse nervously,
not certain his wife would be on the flight.
"These flowers are of significance to us in remembrance,"

he said in flowing Spanish. "Red
is significant for it is the color of passion."

The photo is the first of us as a reunited animal.
How can I describe us? It is not obvious
that his arm bone does not comfortably connect
to her shoulder bone, that my thigh bones
doubt her hip bones, and that her wrist bones wrestle
a strange desire to strike
somebody's, anybody's
head bone. A photographer
hands me a toothpick
with an American flag glued to it.
My mother grabs my hand
instinctively. A bulb explodes. The caption reads,
"Flowers, a flag and a loving touch."

It was the first reunion for Mr. and Mrs. S——
and their 4-year-old daughter
since Argentine police arrested the parents
at their home on Jan. 12, 1977
and imprisoned them on
unspecified charges.
Mrs. S—— commented that she had been kept
in a 9-foot by 9-foot prison cell
for almost three years and thousands
like her are still in prison in Argentina.
"Yesterday was the first time in three years
I have been able to touch my daughter," she said.

I vomited in the clouds
above the ocean
between Buenos Aires and New Orleans,
vomited my grandmother's food
upon my mother's lap.

One stewardess gave me a hard American mint,
red and white, to suck on
and pinned a pair of plastic wings to my chest;
said it was the shock of clouds
that had made me sick.

PORTRAIT OF A FATHER–BAHÍA BLANCA '77

I.

hair on chin, on fingers, on chest,
on legs, on wrists, on arms
on which I rest

smile that opens to eat ten toes or blow umbilical horns
and laugh

ché new man of helping hands,
diaper, food and milk

smell of soap, of sweat, of books, of
mate, wine and cigarettes

sweet night song in deep sad voice duerme
duerme negrita

arms to be hushed and held in

II.

8 break door with boots and guns
throw shelves and drawers and tables on floor
steal books and pictures and papers and poems
and mamá and run and run and
mamá and I no more no more and
one word crawls and looks and looks
papá?

III.

blindfold and number
no air no light
interrogate and break
no air no light
slap and suffocate

8

no air no light
electrocute and rape
no air no light
chain and castrate
no air no light
shoot and sedate
no air no light
kill and negate
no air no light

*what happened to the fathers who were disappeared what happened
to the children what happened to the mothers why don't the men
speak of these things tell me survivor how does it feel to survive how
many endings can I imagine for the poets the high school student the
babies that are all disappeared why bring back the past why
name these things why do you want to know?*

*I have a puzzle missing one piece I have a piece to a puzzle I can't fix
papá?*

O INFAMOUS WINDOW

Abel was gracious to let him in
and to let him sit.
Abel even offered the priest
a demitasse and a cara sucia,
then asked
Where is my son?

The priest smiled:
No sé señor.
And calmly bit
into the sweet-faced pastry
with the carriage
of one who can enter
any home
and partake of the meat
and of the cake
and eat and eat.

The priest licked his fingers
and smiled again:
I had nothing to do with it.
The defect, I'm afraid,
is yours.

Decades later,
Abel would tell his granddaughter
that he rose and roared the priest a curse
louder than the salt-lunged sea lions of Tierra del Fuego.
And to this day no one knows for sure
if the priest was an informant
but what is confirmed
is that one morning
the priest climbed up the steeple
to ring the bells
and . . .

10

well, the priest lived
but with many
broken bones.

●　　●　　●

The first act in the drama of disappearance,
which involved both the victims and their relatives,
began with the sudden bursting into their homes
of the group responsible for the abduction.

From the thousands of testimonies
in the Commission's Files,
we have concluded that these operations,
as part of the use
of kidnapping as a form of detention,
took place at night
or in the early hours of the morning,
and usually towards the end of the week,
so that it would be some time
before the relatives of the person abducted
could take any action.
It was usually a group
of five or six people who forced their way into
homes.†

Every day
in the hours after lunch
I end up knocking at her bedroom door
I knock and knock and knock
after having knocked
on all the other doors of our house
the cabinets the refrigerator
the icebox the closets *mamámamámamá?*

† *Nunca más: The Report of the Argentine National Commission on the Disappeared.*
New York: Farrar, Straus and Giroux/Index on Censorship, 1986, p. 11.

And this is the last door,
the door I know will answer *come in.*
I glide past her galaxy
of gold and silver medals
that place her among painters
in this crooked seaside town.

On her walls I swing wide
atop the nightmare's swings
and the doll that belonged to my mother
swings beside me.
Around us, distorted houses of red and amber
twist high toward purplish skies.
Below us, the umber road shrivels.
It would be a long, long fall
if either of us fell.

I reach the foot of my grandmother's bed
and climb up for a round of play.
She points up and the room fills with astonishing birds.
She challenges me to detect which among these
are predators.
I point to one, two, three,
then I see them all.
Now, she says,
imagine your hands
are guns

•   •   •

Sometimes several different groups were involved,
and in some special cases up to fifty people took part.
The members of the gang always had with them
a weaponry that was totally disproportionate
to the supposed threat posed by the victims.
The gang would threaten them, their families and their neighbours
with both revolvers and heavier weapons.

Often prior to the gang's arrival
the electricity supply to the area
where the raid was being carried out was cut off.
The number of vehicles involved varied.
In some cases, several private cars were used
(usually without license plates) . . .

(Nunca más 11-12)

there were no water fountains or coke machines
in the courtyard waiting area
and most prisoners were called los comunes
because they were common thieves and murderers.

bottom line, sister, their relatives were allowed chairs and shade.

and "courtyard waiting area" is a bit generous
to describe where *we* waited.
we were not there for *los comunes.*

we stood against the endless prison wall,
on the outside, for all the better eyes to watch
our good clothes turn rank,
our clean faces salt.
we hated the eye back.

ask God for water! a guard spat
at a daughter of los subversivos
and there is nothing infantile or hollywood
about why. The longest finger of the crusades.

and so when the hour came, we marched
family per family into the church
that sanctified the prison, and then, out
and straight into the box

where all the demons were kept
and when we were in, we were in
and they closed the door.

●　　●　　●

. . . when members of the regular armed forces were involved,
sometimes in uniform, trucks or vans which could be identified
as belonging to one or other of the forces were brought in.
Occasionally, helicopters circled over the neighbourhood
where the victims lived.

This intimidation and terror was employed
not merely to forestall any possibility
of response by the victims. It was also aimed
at achieving a similar effect on all those living nearby.
Traffic was frequently brought to a halt,
loudhailers, searchlights, bombs and grenades
used in an excessive show of force.

(*Nunca más* 12)

what boy child stood crying in the middle
of the longest sidewalk, the butcher
shop behind him, his grandmother
coaxing—come, come, it's only a cow.

what flies into us fast
and detaches us from the bone:
the carcass in the butcher shop
is after all and yet suddenly
a carcass.

the brains, brains.
the heart, heart.

so what the words:
what it *once* was.

done is the thing done
and what flew into the boy child
on his longest sidewalk ever? what
is that piece of him that opened beyond his cavity
—his heart? no, not his organ nor his soul.
but the sudden knowing
of the thing that has happened

how did it happen

the unspeakable thing.

•   •   •

If the armed assailants did not find their intended victim at home,
they prepared what was known as a 'mousetrap',
and stayed on the spot
until the person they sought
returned.
This led to the kidnapping
going on for many hours
or even days,
with changes in the personnel involved.
In all of these cases the relatives were used
as hostages, and often submitted to brutal pressure and attacks.
The kidnappers would steal all the food and drink they needed,
searching and almost invariably looting the properties.

If anyone happened to come to the house,
they were also taken hostage.
If the originally intended victim did not appear,
the attackers often took away someone else
(a relative or other person
staying in the house at the time).

(Nunca más 15)

She tired of the whole thing running her
into her mother's loveless blue ghost. Blue
and suffocating—like all huge blue space—
wholly oxygenless—and greedy. So,

with the ill patience of a lilac plucked
from a tree, glorious little miracle
maimed, Irene greeted at her table the gray line
of her mother's surviving friends, their children,
human rights investigators and students.

After a few rounds of ritual *mate*
and obviously biased courtesies,
Irene would notice their weepy eyeballs swoop into
her living black hair,
her living cheekbones,
her living black eyes
and she knew the break-in was next,

and out her mouth the words swung hard
"My mother must have done something to deserve it"

And oh
the words
retracted retreated sometimes cold stopped
the weepy sticky taking eyeballs of those who'd come
looking, box of charity pastries in hand, for an extension
of the woman she mirrored exactly,
to speak through her to her.

Oh people come wanting and wanting,
people come to take and take away
with cruelties like photos
and unasked-for anecdotes.

Mad are some ways to keep whole
and like a plucked lilac,
somewhat alive.

• • •

When a family which was to be chupada, had children, the
following methods were employed:

1 *The children were left with neighbours to be looked after until a*
   family relative arrived.
2 *They were sent to children's homes. These would hand them*
   over to relatives or have them adopted.
3 *The children might themselves be abducted and eventually*
   adopted by a member of the armed forces.
4 *They might be taken directly to the victim's relatives, often in the*
   same vehicle used to abduct their parents.
5 *They might be left abandoned in the place from which the group*
   had kidnapped their parents.
6 *They could be taken to the secret detention centre, where they*
   would witness the tortures inflicted on their parents, or they
   might themselves be tortured in front of their parents. Many of
   these children are now among the list of "disappeared".

   (*Nunca más* 14)

Behold an apricot chin,
toddler nostrils,
flared and boogered.
And this one, glossy whites of eyes rolled,
just a quarter moon of honey showing.
Or here, sweetly milk-toothed and swinging on the walnut tree,
and oblivious playing with blue toy blow-dryer
in a box of brown sand.
With each visit he took dozens of them.

They must've thought I would die suddenly.
Or that later my mother would want to see
evidence of my body fine without her body.
Perhaps taking pictures
is the compulsion of memory

17

when memory herself becomes a night-walking
puma on the pulse of buried bones, a slow shimmer
playing you in the fainting light of your brain's huge moon.
Here kitty kitty. Memory has strong incisors.

And it would be a lie to say that love,
after they attacked us, was the cosmic thing
around which we spun closer and closer together.
How much hurt can an equally hurt person love?
I always imagine myself a perpetually frowning thing,
But no.

             •   •   •

Not yet mature adults, adolescents are not children either.
They have not yet taken fundamental decision about life, but
they are beginning to define themselves.
They do not know much about the complexities of politics, and
they have not completed their cultural education.
They are guided by their emotions.
They are not prepared to resign themselves
to the imperfections of a world
inherited from their seniors.
In some an ideal is growing,
an incipient rejection of injustice
and hypocrisy that can make
an anathema of things in a way that is at once
abrupt and ingenuous.
Perhaps, because dramatic changes are going in their own bodies
they reject anything that is presented to them
as unchangeable.

        (*Nunca más* 312)

We huddle, two chilly chickadees,
beneath a blanket to watch the Three Stooges
break out of jail—I break into shivers.

You rise suddenly with another voice
and I am transported to the kitchen.
You batter and bake the shapes
I tell you are in my dreams.
You are strong to bite off their heads and laugh.
You let me wash the dishes with my tongue.

We pick a bouquet of backyard stones and
water them before my naptime. I dream slow.
When you become hollow-bodied music,
I am the green strokes of flowers and grass.
We both have an affinity to birds.

Thank God for fragile weird wings.

•   •   •

The purpose of the first torture sessions was to 'soften up'
newly-arrived prisoners, and these were carried out by any of
the personnel. Once it had been established that the prisoner
had some information of interest to offer, sessions run by special
interrogators began. In other words, there wasn't even a prior
assessment made as to whether the person they were going to
kidnap really knew anything of any interest to his captors.

(*Nunca más* 60)

I don't remember what actually triggered
the insurgence of that day, what set in
motion our little hurricane bodies.

But I do know that together we lost
our teeth and together we learned English
from the TV in the house of exiles

where my father, my stepfather-to-be,
your mother's boyfriend and a bunch of men
we called *tíos* lived and so basically

you and I were destined to be juntas.

Still, who came up with the idea
to lure Colin, our six-year-old neighbor,
over to our side with unsweetened lemon water.

What in our five-year-old bones said jump
then strip Colin of his *Star Wars* T-shirt.
And where did we get the imagination

to then take a steak knife
to my father's bedroom in the basement
and stab the feathers out the pillows that he slept on

and then douse the gutted dream down
with warm orange juice.
Who taught us to turn over his chairs.

Who taught us to empty his drawers.
I found the papers—my father's
birth certificate, prison release forms,
legal U.S. entry and parolee status papers,
all his money.

And I cut them
into the smallest pieces.

Who instructed us to then run
upstairs to the bathroom
with Colin's *Star Wars* shirt still in one of our hands.

I locked the door
and peed in the tub, but you stuffed his shirt
in the toilet and shat.

Then we were quiet
and only our eyes moved.

When my father took me downstairs
for my first and last spanking,
you tried to defend me from him.
But he cried more than me.

•   •   •

Because of these indiscriminate methods, not only members of
armed groups but also their relatives, friends, colleagues at work
or school, political party activists, priests and laymen committed
to the problems of the poor, student activists, trade unionists,
neighborhood leaders and—in a remarkably high number of
cases—people with no kind of trade union or political activity at
all, were rounded up and tortured. It was enough to appear in
somebody's address book to instantly become a target for the
notorious 'task forces'.

(*Nunca más* 60)

Pops tells me in prison he was *Mandíbula*—
The Jaw—the only one able to eat rancid chorizo
tucked in partially molded bread. And once he
told me of a brother taking a noon dump in the latrine.
Pops shouted, "Hey, Bro', what's up!" and bro',
deep in squat hailed back, "Thinking 'bout the revolution,
hermano!" Perhaps Pops has to share this.
We are silent about the day they came;
we are silent about not having fled.
We are silent about what happened to him
inside the death camp. But absurdities are sharable.
He will not share with me the bloody dress
that I invent they dangled before him "this is your daughter"
and still he refused to speak.

．　　．　　．

But the reality was different.
There were thousands of deaths.
None of these came about
through an ordinary or military trial;
none was the result of a sentence.

Technically speaking,
they were murders,
murders into which
no proper investigation
was ever carried out
and for which
those responsible
were never,
as far as we know,
punished
in any way.

To conclude,
the regime
which considered it necessary
to change our legal tradition
by introducing capital punishment,
never used it as such.
Instead
it organized a collective crime,
a veritable mass extermination,
on which the evidence is now
coming to light in the morbid form
of hundreds of nameless corpses
and the testimony of the survivors,
telling of those who died in agony.

(*Nunca más* 209)

One guard in gray specializes in contraband.
She slides her chapped fat hands up my thighs and through
while muttering about your doggishness.
I know I am nothing more than child of a dog to her.

Indescribable it is to be imprisoned,
at least temporarily, with you.

I decide to never understand
the Plexiglas or the infernal not-knowing
which in the row of the waiting women
is you; their eyes and yours
love me equally.

I sit on my grandmother's lap
and bruise her.
No 3-year-old words
exist for this fury.
Here my legs go.

The walls, the walls
on my side and your side
are the same:
the infinite indefinite color
of filth.

And you cannot smell
the shit
on my side
nor the urine
I and the other children do
on the floor in the corners or beside the chairs
that we sit upon to look at you.
We are all locked in—
like dogs—
it is the smell of seeing you I cannot forget.

And I don't remember
one word or story
you ever give me;
I take you home
in pockets no one can seize—
I take you home
with my eyes.

UNSWEETENED

Fresh out of an Argentine prison, what Julio craved most was a
    tortilla.
Having explained his craving, his good host made a list
and promptly returned with canned peas, brown eggs
and a pound of potatoes.

But when he was done with the frying,
the Spanish omelet did not at all taste of salt and earth.
Instead, it tasted sweet. In fact, everything in Seattle
tasted sweet: sweet brown rivers for breakfast, sweet
peanut mush and jam for lunch, sweet jellies and red sauces
on meats for dinner. Julio's host could not imagine the taste
of unsweetened peas, nor the need, but worked to find a can
that would not betray Julio's memory of the simple pea.
Wife still in prison, to taste a pea without sugar—
a natural green pea—became Julio's obsession.
An obsession, which led to strategy: enough English
and enough good host's spare change
to search for *peas, no sugar* on his own.

Nine weeks into the States and host in the meat department,
Julio kneeled at the bottom shelf of the canned food aisle,
picking can after can from row after row of canned peas,
looking for home.

—

II

THE ADVENTURES OF GHETTO GIRL

JUNE 1980

Bert's gigantic yellow conehead hung from a rope, from a tree.
I knew to run when I saw the blindfold and the stick.
But some drunk took me by my wrist to the back of the line
where lil' Che stood first in command, blindfolded and swaggering
from the prerequisite spins. *Down With Berty!* a mother yelled.

When my turn came, the revolutionary who spun me whispered
It's OK, mija, go on now and whack it!
Like some poor-girl therapy, I beat the frown out that uptight
conehead who taught me Buenos Días/Good Morning
Buenas Noches/Good Night.

And I did not know till then that some brains were made of candy,
some hollow heads were better brought down and done with.
Yes, we busted open Bert's head, I delivered the deathblow
and *Órale!* Lil' Dolores yelled when I did.

AT A RALLY FOR THE DISAPPEARED

Ma Sue lifts the megaphone to her lips
and like an emergency room doctor, jolts
the circular body of 200 legs into motion—
¡El pueblo unido, jamás será vencido!
At the center of this circling body,
the 6 and under sit in plain view
of our mothers. We know to share
what food and toys our pockets hold.
Some of us wear extra-small slogans
across our chests and others, like me,
are dressed churchlike. I lie back
in my orange-flowered brown dress
and lift my ankle socks to the hot blue
sky to relieve my legs of gravel burn
when accidentally I topple our jumbo-size collective cup of water.
Ma Sue's son closes his eyes
and whispers above our puddle of misfortune,
but the water does not respond.

GEOMETRY

Before my mother runs away
with my father's housemate
on a Greyhound,
leaving me behind,
this time voluntarily
but to her credit, temporarily,
she will host parties
where wine will agree
to forever follow solitude
in this and that one's vessel,
where blue bellbottoms will
hustle and for old times, twist,
and I will ignore the dancers
and stand on a chair
before a night-fevered window,
drawing slow unstable circles.

PAPI'S AFRO PICK

Papi gives me sourdough toast with sour cream
for breakfast every day and this summer I can
put on orange socks and green pants by myself.
I tell him I even know how to brush my own
hair and show him how: lightly passing the brush over
the top of my head, slicking back rebel naps
into the ponytail Ma made for me before I boarded
the plane. I lie, *Ma siempre lets me do my hair.*

One day, Reina and I are looking at ourselves
in the José Martí Daycare bathroom mirror,
sharing pineapple lip gloss and contraband sweets,
when suddenly, she gasps and digs two tan fingers
into the same ponytail Ma made for me six weeks
ago. We *oooooh* and *daaaaang* as she holds up
thick long clumps of hair for me to see in the mirror.
She finds another clump, two clumps then three. *Just like
chorizos!* she whispers. When Pa sees this he cries
¡Ay carajo! then calls my aunt Mara who comes over
with a comb and 3 bottles of Vidal Sassoon
the brand we can trust she says. But after soaking
my chorizo clumps for one hour in our trusty cream,
my know-it-all-aunt can't undo one single knot
and throws in her towel: *Julio, there's no hope for her.*
Before giving up the chorizo wars, Pa enlists his girlfriend
from Detroit, who takes one look and laughs *That ain't never
coming out . . . She's got your hair, Julio.* Pa sits down
on the dirty carpet, back turned, head bowed
what-will-your-mother-think-of-me. I stand behind him
holding his unbreakable black steel pick.

BROWN-EYED NIECE

he was my father like my father
died when I was
he was my friend like my friend
died when I was
he was my brother like my brother
died when I was
he was my uncle like
father
brother
friend

he died when I was o I can't say his name
his name was
he died when I was
and I was just so
his name was
he died
his name
my
father
brother
uncle
friend
died and I
o yes his name
his name was like the song
Didn't My Lord Deliver
yes his name was
Daniel

he died when I was o he died yesterday when I was 9
he died when I was so big I had him in my brains and bones already
he died yesterday he really did my uncle brother father friend
How he die? How he die? How did your unclebrotherfatherfriend
die?

They killed him
They killed him
Suicide
your brother uncle father friend ! ? girl, stop telling lies!
123456789
when I was 1 before I was 2
he become brother
father
uncle
friend
he taught me to put color on paper and pencils in their place
he shrank so tiny like me we
pretended to be dolls and birds
I grew so tall like him we
spoke and anyway
what size is love and what size do friends come in

HARDY MIDDLE SCHOOL, GEORGETOWN

they call me nasty and smelly
because spanish men piss and blow snot
right onto sidewalk and street,
they call me spanish and poor
but the names I can't say are the worst.
one day I was doing the butt
and the buck wild on the basketball court
when rozanne who's half
puerto rican whispers: girl,
get a morena perm
—I open my locker and find
a pencil sketch of a girl
big head, crossed eyes,
flat nose, tongue out and black
ink exploding on the head,
black ink
grabbed hard and pressed down harder
coiling
angry and quick
all over the page,
tight black twists
sloppy and slipping
off the white sheet,
an explosion!
an explosion!
a fierce
make little
black pieces
explosion
I scream
Mistake!
inside my head
then see my name
turn just in time
to catch

six blonde
reebok & benetton
girls
laughing, perfumed
and
running away.

LAS A-E-I-O-U'S DE LOS UMS SEEKING TONGUES OF MIGRATIN' LETRAS QUE AIN'T NO WAY HIDING

1.

gyrating spanglish verses in the rundown where dominicans loved
and I watched in a city so black
they call it chocolate
is the root
word
behind this eloquence.
yo elaboraré on every detail para que usted
tenga la oportunidad to fully comprehend
the logistics of
mi latina
oral stream.

2.

The fortunetellers in the den of thieves predict the future:
the temperature is changing
due to a warm front sweeping in from the south,
south of the equator,
all of Miami and east of L.A.
Actually, the ravage of tropical storm
TwoTongue LenguaFresca
has been taking its toll on these
southern areas
for a few centuries now
with the surfacing of a dark and mysterious disease.
The exotic natives of these lands were the first
to show symptoms of this disease
that, according to doctors and some medicine men,
is acquired in the rare instance
that the YoNoSpeakNoInglesh Virus
comes in contact with U.S. borders or shores.
Consequently, these inhabitants were also

the first
to show signs of immunity to this malady,
as their tongues
developed a thick coat of repellent,
resistant to psychologically induced
OneTongueAntibodies.
Though officials sought to quarantine
those unfortunates
afflicted with this debilitating
enfermedad, excuse me, I mean disease,
we now have report
that a new strain of this grave condition
has been found spreading
through most metropolitan and urbanized areas
throughout the country.
This new strain, like the previous bug,
is being attributed to the radical climatic change
triggered by a warm front sweeping in
from a new southern region,
the South Bronx.
However, amid the ensuing panic,
we must remember that this disease
is completely preventable.
All that is required to protect you
and your loved ones from catching this disease
is to remain celibate from any form of unbiased cultural
intercourse.
In the case that such intercourse becomes inevitable,
don't think, simply be closed minded—
lack of communication is crucial.
Remind your infected partner that
he/she should go home;
be sure to specify that you mean Mexico,
or if he/she is black,
you might want to suggest Puerto Rico.
Do not compromise your ignorance; remain firm
in forbidding the presence of any infected individual

amidst the company of you and your family.
Help the community—support intolerance
donate votes to abolish bilingualism.
Spread the word against the disease at your workplace
by promoting mandatory acculturation and random tongue
searches.
Be sure to report any suspicious dialect behavior
and seize all forms of deviant rhetoric.
Promote Safe Assimilation.
With your help, we can stop the spread of this disease.
Remember the INS is on your side.
This has been María Rosa García López
reporting en vivo, I mean quise decir,
live from America.

3.

i ain't denyin' nothin'
i'm a contradiction
in itself
an' this
is how I SPEAK so listen y escuchalo bien
cuz you know how I be feelin'
'bout repitiendome
tu ves, es que
this is what I have become
ha ha ha
I laugh at all the
pimp mack daddy hos hooker dope crack feign perverted greasy
head big tit mami rosa maría holy jesus jose superfly coke dealing
rapist mammies maids pea brained
illiterates
projected on the screen
cuz we resemble,
you know what I mean?
she always look like me
and at times,

if they did a lot of anthropological research
they even master the sound of we

4.

In college I am
an English major
thus,
fully capable of expressing
clarity of thought
in the properness of textbook
fashion, *shit*,
I mean, furthermore, I can
assess your own thoughts, so do not think too loud . . . yes yesss
you grapple with
spics, us spanish folk who sho loves to
talk like dat . . . ¡arriba arriba ándale ándale!
but does it scare you
to know that
in the privacy
of our own homes
of our own minds
many sp, pardon me, latinos,
you know the *good ones,*
who've bachelored
and mastered the white
eloquence
of *proper* English,
speak this urban and rural
broke up and to'up
southern and backward
norteño and forward
speech?
and that you can't understand
or even pretend like you do?
how does it feel to be left out and out
of control?

it must feel like
time for some action
some good legal action and moral
enforcing time for some national
head banging tongue lynching
and
none of it works—
we
just
can't
seem
to get
the fucking picture.

5.

we speak
this tree of tongued jewels
from which origins seep forth;
like a brook in a forest
we gurgle the isms of recurring nightmares and
like the earth we decompose
shackles into vital minerals.

listen,
you will hear
staggering languages
of crossed oceans
crutched by seashells held to ears.
so natural, our tongues be
free of constraints
in a land where living
on earth has a fee and we are
a national nightmare realized
by the influx of aliens
encountering in-a-city realities,
copulating lenguas entre labios, creating

spoken masterpieces with fluid affinity;
displaced immigrant words
become spoken refugees
as blackboards give birth
to the ya tu sabes whats up.

6.

recuerdo yo
mi primer paso
un día
a grip of years ago
en mi school
can't you see it
ooh ooh teacha look it
we took a problem and resolved it
entre los morenos
y los dominicanos
each was forced to choose
and i thought well coño fuck it
being la tremenda smartass que soy yo
i'm a let the teacher know
that i speak the reflection of where i'm from
i mirror the voices from the drone
now, she said i spoke broken
the language of the broke
the black and the foreign
so i asked her
but how bright could we be
to take two languages and make them three

7.

let me continue
que quisiera brindar
la elocuencia
de nuestra realidad
es muy simple

en su complejidad.
I scream you scream
the grandiose immigrant dream
between heaven and earth
like limbo we steam
in praise of language
sweet words from the soul
furiously spoken
this tongue is
as rebellious as freedom
and we speak
in slave tongues
that gum
drop stick
to the air like
the pollution
of dust
a filmy darkness
that envelops us
across the land
grammar book anarchy
is at hand.

AFTER SCHOOL

I scurry to some safe part
of wall when floodlights come
and they come like a man certain
small things in his house
eat his private bread. I am
the floodlight's cockroach. I can die
on contact. I scurry off the bus down
the street up the stairs after 3
and into the tub made of steel safer
than windows for scrawling
basic math, one day plus one day plus one.

AT THE D.C. MULTIPLEX

ghetto girl
not your average super heroine
flyin' higher
than most
wonder women

I arrive unannounced
creepin' stealthily
through the boroughs
catchin' every criminal slip
of your tongue
trappin' and slappin'
your ignorance
with my brown
cape

this is no super joke
I have my super crew
and we're coming
to a theater near you
to rescue
all the spics and niggas
stuck in naked freeze frames
big butt monkey sex scenes
illiterate dope dealin' rice and beans
stereotypes
in
stereo sound

hold tight
Rositas, Marías
Josés and Carlitos
Shaquishas, Rasheedas
Big Buck and Sweet Daddy Oooo's

no longer will you have to
likes it like dis or loves it like dat baby

yeah

I'm ghetto girl
and
I'm coming
to a theater near you

EL BUS 42

mornings from
September to June
we walked like
badass bulldozers
to the back
of the bus, far from
our mothers,
the word was didit
or fucked the
word was bitch ho my
man bought me
that thing you want. word.
who kept count
of the homemade things
that left our
wombs sucked dry or dead?
we didn't know
we were fragile
on our way from one war
to the next.

THE RELAX

After fuckin in a public bathroom, a parking lot,
my best friend's bed, a shower, a park,
a couch, a floor, he calls me phat with a kiss
as in pussy hips ass and tits.

Yo soy 18 & Igetmyhairdonewithmy *own* money,
honey.

Champaign does my hair.
She morena but light skinded like me,
almost white, when she saw me she was like
I'll make your hair Chinese.
So she put on the cream and told me *relax.*

I'll admit,
It burned a bit
then it burned like hell
but I kept my cool
and when Champaign was done,
girl, it lay so flat you couldn't tell
'cept for the scabs on my head
and the blood on my scalp
that I ever had had
a curl on my head.

SAINT LIGHT-SKINNED SEÑORITA

". . . in college I knew a girl from Argentina.
I spoke to her in Spanish
but she never spoke back . . ."
the lawyer declares
before plunging her fingers
into my hair.
Sin satisfied,
the lawyer feels strangely
clean then remembers
"may I touch?"
but, alas, statues don't speak
so I spoke not a word.
And the lawyer left
beset with dry tongue
and the imprint of wool,
forever itching
the palm of her hand.

The second lawyer comes in,
confesses: *"One time*
for Halloween,
I painted myself
black
and put on
an afro wig.
But I have a friend
from the Caribbean
who looks a lot like you,
who just laughed and laughed
when I told her
about Halloween."
I tell her: Tell this story
to every person
of color
you know,

tell it to them
all the time.
You must
face the looks
you make.

The last lawyer of the day tells me he likes watching the Spanish
channel. He says it's really good.
Although he doesn't understand any Spanish,
the long Indian hair and bare tits say it all.
I tell him: When you least expect it, you will dance
naked through the streets of New Jersey
and Indian hair women will laugh, their laughter
will say it all.

I close the curtain for the day. And sharpen my blade.
All around me I hear:
"O Bilingual Paralegal intervening between two worlds,
light-skinned vessel, gratuitous confessional before you
I kneel and repent my funny thing
or just tell the truth about what I think.
O Light-Skinned Señorita! hallow be thy name,
NOT LIKE THE OTHERS you are called.
May your fairness multiply.
May you be The One
to receive first dibs
and the itty bitty crumb
less traffic tickets
and THE BENEFIT of THE DOUBT.
Holy lightened lamb of the dark past,
Intervene on our behalf
and have mercy on our skins."

MILAGRO

Dulce Milagro of East Orange
admits only one at a time and locks her door.

One at a time, she bends
a weary head back
into agua de rosa
then gently works soft wool
with garlic and aloe, honey, hemp and rum.

Dulce Milagro of East Orange
admits only one at a time and locks her door.

One at a time, she bends
a weary head back
into agua de lila
then gently works loose cotton
with lemon, olive oil and sage.

Dulce Milagro of East Orange
admits only one at a time and locks her door.

One at a time, she bends
a weary head back
into agua de lluvia
then gently works raw silk
with seaweed and mud, placenta and crushed mother of pearl.

One at a time, she bends
a weary head back
below a constellation
of burgundy hearts that hang
from her *Bella Quisqueya* ceiling,
each a love note lettered in gold:

God make beauty,
I am servant of God.

God make natural,
I use natural ingredient.

Guineo, mamey,
leche y miel.

Please don't complain
about how slow I take.

Smile you beauty that way.

III

CAN WE RECONCILE?

LIGHTSKIN MAMBO

what a genetic mambo we got in the garden, wild flower.
we got this kind and that kind in the same soil and water,
all of it a series of conscious decisions
on where to plant and who to cross with.

I did not like your petals at first, too much white.

but you wrote manifestos on brown
paper napkins 'bout working till your bones hurt,
your momma and her slippers upside your head,
hunger and Boriken. I loved you after that,

then I was ashamed. I hated it—our light skin.
like I could have done better, gotten my self browner, saved myself
this way.

all them sweet good names:
trigueña, mulata, blanquita,
negrita, morena, canela, are all laced
with some kind of whip and noose,
some kind of real deep hate
all over us.

baby, the garden is sick.
how we negotiate this hair, those eyes, that skin.
always undoin' something some parent did,
always undoin' something done to them,
always running home or running away
with each lick and gasp of skin. oh the praying we do for this
texture, that tone when all is said and done and the baby is about
to be born. we love like we are investment still. careful who we spit
and kiss as if all this engineering and careful selection will deliver
us. some claim it does, but mostly we just get crazier. it's not

predictable. just look at it—our garden.
baby you know love is a mean mother
when we get picky about her fruit.

WHAT

You are right
I've never been lonely like you
never been alone in a kitchen with 7 brothers
3 sisters 2 mothers a daughter a husband and his 2 friends
a pot of black beans
a pot of hominy
a pot of tamales
a hot comal and 60 tortillas
2 chairs   a big table and a hologram of Jesus above the door
(the one that if you look at him from one angle
he is an intact white man—but if you make a move
his mouth drops eyes roll back and blood gushes from his head)
and the small plastic statue of the Virgen de Guadalupe
plugged in and flashing on off on off
on the kitchen counter
next to the food processor
and the molcajete
and when you cry
everyone believes
it's the onion.

AMIGAS FOREVER

well, these crows are hard to get out my house,
and you, girl, are the worst. where'd you get your hunger
to watch me so?

look how your claws take hold of my crown,
how your talons curl inside my skull,
look how your beak rips out my hair,
pick-peck-pick-peck.
look how you swallow my brainsoulbrain, listen how you caw
whyyougowhyyougowhyyougoaway
look how you hold
      hold
      holdfast in me,
pick-peck-pick-peck possessive bird
oh my, the beauty of your wings and of the old
but the weight and the weight
of being owned.

ORDER!

You come from a family
Of martyrs, real and imagined,
Who condemn the slightest indulgence
In selfish behavior.

I come from a family
Of superheroes, real and imagined,
Who expose the hidden treachery
Behind seemingly innocent acts.

The toilet seat is up.
Long hair clogs the shower drain.

Court is now in session.

THIS DIAMOND IS ROUGH

two hungry stars
consuming bodies of fire
our tongues unrestrained

come fall with wild wind
big belly sun catches us
we are tying knots

invite the people
we will dance our promise words
they will witness us

15.

you make me sing
your anti colonial song
love is political

13.

oye tú, give me whole
passion, crave my sound
deep listen me like jazz

3.

I got me these four babies
And a poem to write
Get your ass home quick

8.

my passion is less
important than food and sex
I don't give you 'nuff

when I go write you
become suddenly injured
hungry and horny

5.

between slap and fuck
you bastard/bitch our love is
good at wanting more

11.

I know you well
We share persecution songs
Our blues keep us bound

10.

tranquilizers
night wine noon whisky morning rye
love has come to this

1.

I write you write we
griots finding home at last
our love poem has come

in this new body
what will happen to our words?

A TREE IN PERTH AMBOY

last spring,
they cut off 3 arms,
left her two.

this spring,
two arms bloom
at dawn, full green.

now, they saw two arms
then shave her—
a living stump between cement.

the birds, 300 spring birds,
trill at the emergency. my plants stiffen
at attention, i close the windows,
but they angle their main leaves
and hear the sound.

now, a pale umber oblong stick,
hits her first and final beat,
but there is no leather,
copper or even some earth
to receive her death song,
only cement street.
her death weight is heavy.
her sound, the hollow sound
of drum with no skin.

my house shakes,
my sofa shakes,
i shake. she is gone,
she is fed into the grinder,
the birds are silent.

ON THE BIRD THAT INTERRUPTED OUR *MATE* AND PASTELILLOS DE GUAYABA

We agree that surely
the shrieking 2 ounces of bone,
flesh and lime-yellow feathers
that has landed
upon our rusted chain link fence
has escaped
not only the cage
but complete
ownership.

> *That bird is not from here,*
> *it will return now,*
you say, sipping on mate,
> *back to its homeland*
> *back to Puerto Rico.*

I swallow the last of the pastelillos
and offer the canary a palm of oily sunflower seeds
from our open living room window:
> *It is good that it does not trust human hands,*
I say and shut the window.

It shrieks uncontrolled
not the green love song his ancestors sang
before the coming of the Spanish
nor the captive melancholy sung in
all the cages thereafter
but a wild-wing-growing
finallyfinally
finally sound.

TEN

1.

Walking off the subway up the ramp through the turnstile up the
steps to the street,
I inhale
I am relieved today does not stink like September,
the wind hardly moves
the smell
Each day I walk onto West 4th, I hold my breath rejecting the stench
of fire
Today it is warm, there is no odor, maybe winter will be
gentle

2.

Regardless of season
Killing is never mild

3.

When the President of the University publicly proclaimed
we were genetically defective, we learned our history quick

We looked to ancestors and took sides

Three years later I see you again
Taped to a wall
"Javier my son, he wear class ring"

4.

When the President of the United States publicly proclaimed war,
I thought of all the homeland terror and genocide that went into
making us immigrants, into making us racially, all the homeland
terror and genocide that didn't want you to wear a class ring
historically and as we speak and at all costs and by any means
and I knew you would have opposed this.

5.

today is bright yellow
like spring or fall beginning

a bridge between fire and snow

you one of the thousands upon thousands
remind me how fragile passing time is

6.

urgent need
to talk
panic
to touch
you alive
I cannot rest
there is blood everywhere

7.

The pigeons in New York are missing pieces of themselves
What's going on? They walk urgently
Between human feet. I have never seen humans
Fly, we are afraid of airplanes we are afraid of heights.

8.

The pigeons in Seattle are lean and glide
With grace alongside the gulls
Perhaps the fish and fruit and ample sky
Keep them healthy

They trust too much and sometimes
We throw alka-seltzer in the air
And watch them gracefully swoop
Down to catch our offerings

With their best pirouette and we watch
Them fly away until they explode inside
And crash like rocks onto the sidewalk

9.

the pigeons in D.C. are different
in Mt. Pleasant there is a park
we call El Parque de las Ratas

first people
then the rats then the pigeons
eat the trash

sometimes crossing El Parque
my sister and I would be hungry
I would say I know what we can do
let's kill that pigeon and eat it.
sometimes she was too hungry to laugh.

10.

to be honest with you
I don't care how pigeons live or think,
I'm really thinking how
paloma means pigeon
and paloma means dove
how dove symbolizes peace
but pigeon is a ubiquitous element of the human landscape
and how the two meanings
are not synonymous
in this language

NOW FOR THE EVENING NEWS

Tonight we continue
Our ongoing look
At terror here, terror there
Terrorism everywhere
As antiwar protestors terrorize the nation
Terror expert Terrence Defort
Presents an inside investigation on
How to attack
A terrorist
Before
A terrorist
Attacks you
But first we turn
To Teresa Terrelle who took
A special look
At the Latino community
And the steps these people
Are taking to prevent
The terrorist from within,
Teresa . . .
           . . . Thank you, Terry

Because they look
Like Islam runs
In their veins
They must say
Their last names
Louder
Shave their beards
And bleach their black
Till the bodegas run
Out of Barbasol
And Revlon

I asked this young man what he thought:
"MY NAME IS JOSÉ, MY NAME IS JOSÉ RODRÍGUEZ, MY NAME
IS NOT MUHAMMAD, MY NAME IS JOSÉ RODRÍGUEZ FROM THE
BRONX"

In response to such fearless response
The National Rules for Hispanic
Has just omitted clause U.S.CLAUSE#1
NEVER MENTION WHERE YOU COME FROM
A new clause requires all Hispanics
To explicitly explain they are Hispanic
With a careful note
To never mention the Moors

A woman whose husband was saved by the new clause had this to
say:
"jes, my hosban was at work, an four coworkers approach him an say
'ju a fokin moslem mudder fokin terroris' and my hosban he so
smart so he say 'no ju wrong man, I'ma latin' an my hosban and he
coworkers star laughin . . . is ok now"

Terry,
Terrorism hits
Very close to home
For these people
Most of whom were born
In terror breeding
Countries like Nicaragua
And El Salvador,
Columbia and Cuba,
Compton and North Korea
Many say they've come to this country
Not to make money but to escape
Terrorists

Mr. Marco, the mayor of the local barrio, concludes the report
with this promise:
"We're working 'round the clock to stop terrorists dead in their tracks
We've gotten a lot of support from the locals who don't mind
Being stopped and interrogated for their safety
And I think it's safe to say that under these circumstances,
The people can be your worst enemy
And your best friend, however, we are encouraged
By the anti-terrorist messages coming from the youth
Who these days aren't being caught dead
Wearing the flags of their foreign mothers and fathers
Instead they are wearing the latest t-shirts that say
'I'm coming to get you, you terrorist' or 'I kick terrorist ass'
It's really heart warming and I'd like to mention
That we have opened a special INS Terrorist Unit in town and
Anyone who suspects their neighbor, teacher, or co-worker is a
Terrorist can report them. On behalf of all the Latins across the land
Let me add we are eager to prove once and for all
That we can be friendly neighbors and good citizens too"

Now, back to you, Terry.

ON RECONCILIATION

Not hard for the tongue to tell salt from candy
or wine from vinegar   but hard
for brain and memory.   I eat bowls of salt,
pop vinegar bottles and laugh, laugh, laugh
but the sun won't crawl from you—
won't nothing warm come to me since birth.

not hard to tell when you are fire but hard
to tell when you're   nonspecific coal.
coo   I would love to baby bird you or mammal up
like that first feeding of flesh upon flesh—
would love to take from you like this,
metaphorically.

but hard for guilt to discern
enemy from anyone, easier to twist
the umbilical into vengeful rope.

ON RECONCILIATION #2

We take the telephone in our kitchens for granted
as if prison microphones
like the cold moon,
      relatively close and visible but
      impossible to touch with hands unbound,
I mean with bare hands,
I mean without glass or metal,
did not lay some gravity upon our tongues—
I mean censorship and loss of love.

I say, we take planes & extra house keys
as if permission paper and visit denied
are forgettable, and the promises forged
in cold cells and on lone swings do not need
to fly, enter a house and speak, simply
and from a place the moon can not touch.

ON RECONCILIATION #3

Bless the open doors. Many have warmed us in,
mic'd up our brokenness, listened
and built for us the human home—we.
And this is enough. Like what sex is,
occasionally one will offspring
action or transformation
in consequence of the contact—
but that is all, that is all. Don't ask
me to reconcile with those who have
sought to kill me, my mother, my father.
Progress depends on more than forgiving.
No. There is no "other way" I must consider.
There is the door. Your door even. You walk,
and befriend and forgive whom you must.

ON RECONCILIATION #4

I am much too much of a mocosa for you.
Behold my defect—
I delay writing cruel girls off.
Worse, I call them Friend
long into the dysfunction, and then
I why? their meanness;
this one ate with everyone but me
and this one said this awful thing
about how I must repent
for what I have done to her
and I swear I did nothing!
Nothing! But note her brilliance,
her strength—an onyx, a tiger's eye!
Why am I her toilet water? I love them so.

But what I don't call you crying about is
how I abandon them all—unexpectedly
in the middle of them needing me most;
how I suddenly realize: this is envy,
and that, self absorption.
And the other, a form of psychological torture—
and usually, while I shower them off my skin, I fight you
about your animal, solidarity. You are the thousandth whore.
And I am your daughter. So, to whom are we honestly and
sacrificially loyal? Somos bestias. Our tiny banners tell us we are
beasts of limited power motivated by the great feeling.

ON RECONCILIATION #5

I would transform
helicopters
into seed
and nectar loving
birds colored lilac
wholly un-evil
you infinitely heavier
than their mass—

with the spin of giant
sunflower stalk
over your head
voilà

HIJA

I am the daughter of doves
That disappeared into dust

Hear my pulse whisper:
>*progre-so*
>*justi-cia*
>*progre-so*
>*justi-cia*

I have many friends and thirty thousand
Warrior angels to watch
Over my exiled skin.

Look what occupies the four chambers of my heart:
>re/vo/lu/ción

You will know me by this.
I am the daughter that never forgets.

A DECEMBER DREAM OF HOUSE AND BIRDS

The House has a ceiling of wood,
and despite the absence of walls,
it remains dark inside.
In one corner of the House
is a round side table,
on which a lamp and a worn,
leather-bound book rest.

How they long to rest.
Instead, they stand.
Each arm wrapped
around another arm,
each head facing west,
watching the birds.

Once upon a time,
a few dozen birds arrived,
and the people figured they could stand
how the birds rearranged their walkways
and so they turned their faces.

Now there are a million birds.

A million pairs of wings
shoot across the sea.
And near the clouds,
they open their bellies
and from their open bellies,
a rosary of people
chained at wrist and ankle
tumble to the water.
O Mother. The People Full of Grace.
Sad and Holy Sea. The wicked birds
and their bloody wings.

The talons the bullets the talons the ropes
the neck the feet the wrist
the talons electric
prod on gums
testicle anus vagina
the talons that yank
people off street in daylight
children off school bus
and never return flesh intact.
Oh the foul foul talons.

Now, the birds storm the House
And fly around the side-table.
They take the book for evidence.
But more important is the brain,
the imagination, the skin,
the human insistence on recreating.

The birds lower their flight to take them.

Ruth Irupé Sanabria's work has appeared or is forthcoming in *Are All the Women Still White? Globalizing Women's Studies; U.S. Latino Literature Today* (2004); *CALYX, A Journal of Art and Literature by Women* (2004); *Long Shot* (2004); *Women Writing Resistance* (2004); *Poets Against the War* (2003); *Coloring Book: An Eclectic Anthology by Multicultural Writers* (2003); and many more. She has performed her work at various venues in the United States, Peru, and Mexico and has worked as a creative writing instructor throughout New York and New Jersey. She lives in Perth Amboy, New Jersey, with her husband and two children. *The Strange House Testifies* is her first book-length collection of poems.